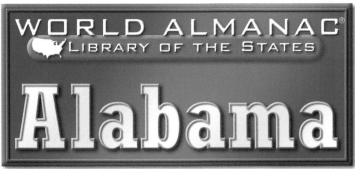

WORLD ALMANAC® LIBRARY OF THE STATES

Alabama

THE HEART OF DIXIE

by Michael A. Martin

Curriculum Consultant: Jean Craven,
Director of Instructional Support,
Albuquerque, NM, Public Schools

WORLD ALMANAC® LIBRARY

Please visit our web site at: **www.worldalmanaclibrary.com**
For a free color catalog describing World Almanac® Library's
list of high-quality books and multimedia programs, call
1-800-848-2928 (USA) or 1-800-387-3178 (Canada).
World Almanac® Library's fax: (414) 332-3567.

Library of Congress Cataloging-in-Publication Data

Martin, Michael A.
    Alabama, the heart of Dixie / by Michael A. Martin.
        p. cm. — (World Almanac Library of the states)
    Includes bibliographical references and index.
    Summary: Presents the history, geography, people, politics and government, economy,
social life and customs, state events and attractions, and notable people of Alabama.
        ISBN 0-8368-5127-7 (lib. bdg.)
        ISBN 0-8368-5297-4 (softcover)
        1. Alabama—Juvenile literature. [1. Alabama.] I. Title. II. Series.
    F326.3.M27   2002
    976.1—dc21   2002069116

This edition first published in 2002 by
World Almanac® Library
330 West Olive Street, Suite 100
Milwaukee, WI 53212 USA

This edition © 2002 by World Almanac® Library.

Design and Editorial: Bill SMITH STUDIO Inc.
Editor: Kristen Behrens
Assistant Editor: Megan Elias
Art Director: Olga Lamm
Photo Research: Sean Livingstone
World Almanac® Library Project Editor: Patricia Lantier
World Almanac® Library Editors: Monica Rausch, Jim Mezzanotte, Mary Dykstra
World Almanac® Library Production: Scott M. Krall, Tammy Gruenewald,
  Katherine A. Goedheer

Photo credits: pp. 4-5 © Alabama Bureau of Tourism&Travel/Dan Brothers; p. 6 (top right)
© Corel, (bottom right) © PhotoDisc; p. 7 (top) © Gabriel Benzur/TimePix, (bottom) © PhotoDisc;
p. 9 © Francis G. Mayer/CORBIS; p. 10 © ArtToday; p. 11 © Dover; p. 12 © Bettmann/CORBIS;
p. 13 © Alabama Bureau of Tourism&Travel/Dan Brothers; p. 14 NASA; p. 15 © Don
Cravens/TimePix; p. 17 © Margaret Bourke-White/TimePix; p. 18 © Richard Cummins/CORBIS;
p. 20 (all) © Alabama Bureau of Tourism&Travel/Dan Brothers; p. 21 (left) © Alabama Bureau of
Tourism&Travel/Karim Basha, (middle) © Corel, (right) © PhotoDisc; p. 23 © Alabama Bureau
of Tourism&Travel/Karim Basha; p. 27 © Huntsville Convention & Visitor's Bureau; p. 29
© PhotoDisc; p. 31 © Bill Eppridge/TimePix; p. 32 © Mobile CVB; p. 33 (top) © Huntsville
Convention & Visitor's Bureau, (bottom) © Huntsville Convention & Visitor's Bureau; p. 34
© Alabama Bureau of Tourism&Travel/Karim Basha; p. 35 © Alabama Bureau of Tourism&
Travel/Karim Basha; p. 36 © TimePix; p. 37 © Alabama Bureau of Tourism&Travel/Karim Basha;
p. 38 © Dover Publications; p. 39 (top) © Dover Publications, (bottom) © Library of Congress;
p. 41 (top left) © Artville, (right) NASA; pp. 42-43 © Library of Congress; p. 44 (top) © PhotoDisc,
(bottom) © PhotoDisc; p. 45 © Auburn/Opelika CVB/Robert Smith

Printed in the United States of America

1 2 3 4 5 6 7 8 9 06 05 04 03 02

Alabama

A Land in Transition

A labama is filled with unique natural treasures as well as rich historical and cultural traditions. The state is home to a wide variety of natural environments, from mountains to forests to ocean shorelines. Humans have enjoyed Alabama's beautiful and varied landscape ever since the region first became home to hunter-gatherers some twelve thousand years ago. In more recent times, Alabama has been many things to many people. Throughout the eighteenth and nineteenth centuries, "King Cotton," the state's dominant cash crop, shaped the region. Montgomery, Alabama's capital, later became known as "the Cradle of the Confederacy," serving as a center of political activity and power for the southern states whose withdrawal from the Union in 1861 touched off the Civil War. The state's abundant natural resources have made it a leader in U.S. steelmaking. In addition, Alabama engineers and scientists played vital roles in sending U.S. astronauts to the Moon.

The state has given the world its fair share of influential people and history-makers. Among the famous names Alabama has produced are pioneering African-American agricultural chemist George Washington Carver; author, lecturer, and advocate Helen Keller; world heavyweight boxing champion Joe Louis; African-American educator and social reformer Booker T. Washington; and country music legend Hank Williams.

During the 1960s, Alabama became the flash point for the Civil Rights Movement, focusing national attention on the injustices endured by African Americans. The Civil Rights Act of 1964 was passed largely because of the efforts of dedicated activists — such as Dr. Martin Luther King, Jr. — who worked tirelessly to improve race relations in Alabama and throughout the nation. Much social progress has been made since then, brightening the outlook for Alabama's future.

▶ Map of Alabama showing the interstate highway system, as well as major cities and waterways.

▼ Johnny's Creek runs through Little River Canyon.

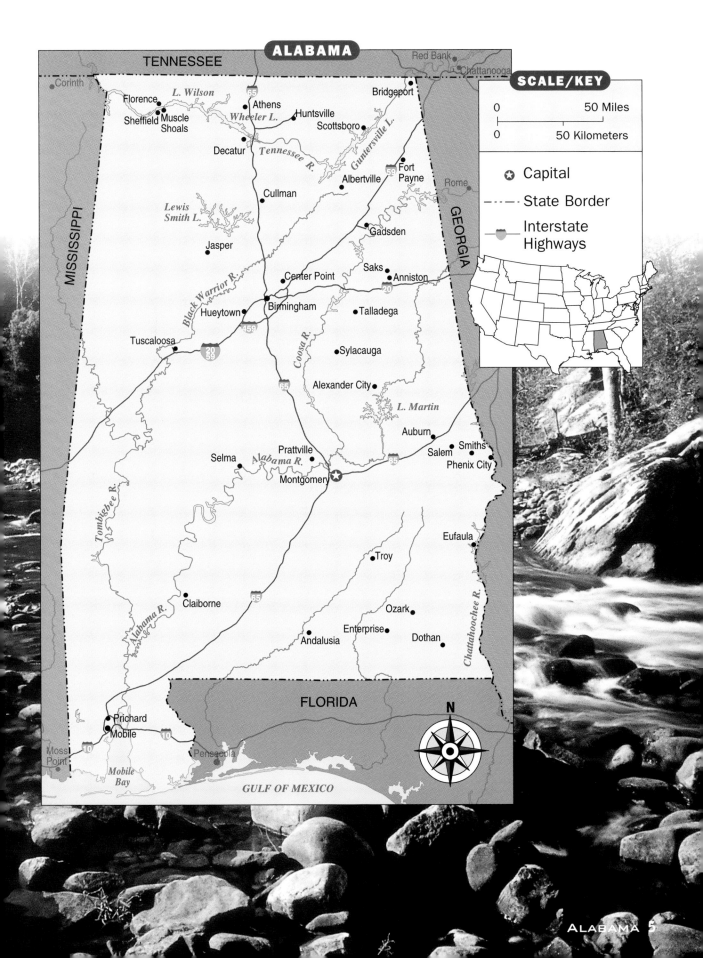

TENNESSEE

Red Bank

Chattanooga

SCALE/KEY

| 0 | 50 Miles |
| 0 | 50 Kilometers |

⭐ Capital

–··–··– State Border

🛡 Interstate Highways

Corinth

Florence
Sheffield Muscle Shoals

L. Wilson
Athens
Wheeler L.
Huntsville
Scottsboro

Bridgeport

Guntersville L.

Decatur
Tennessee R.

Fort Payne

Rome

GEORGIA

Cullman
Albertville

Lewis Smith L.

Gadsden

Jasper

Saks
Anniston

Center Point
Black Warrior R.

Birmingham
Hueytown

Talladega

Tuscaloosa

Coosa R.

Sylacauga

Alexander City

L. Martin

MISSISSIPPI

Auburn

Selma
Alabama R.
Prattville
Montgomery

Salem
Smiths
Phenix City

Tombigbee R.

Eufaula

Troy

Claiborne
Alabama R.

Ozark
Enterprise
Andalusia
Dothan

Chattahoochee R.

FLORIDA

N

Prichard
Mobile

Moss Point

Pensacola

Mobile Bay

GULF OF MEXICO

Fast Facts

Alabama (AL), Heart of Dixie

Entered Union

December 14, 1819 (22nd state)

Capital	Population
Montgomery	201,568

Total Population (2000)

4,447,100 (23rd most populous state)

Largest Cities	Population
Birmingham	242,820
Montgomery	201,568
Mobile	198,915
Huntsville	158,216

Land Area

50,744 square miles (131,427 square kilometers) (28th largest state)

State Motto

"We Dare Defend Our Rights"

State Song

"Alabama," *lyrics by Julia Strudwick Tutwiler and music by Edna Gockel Gussen, adopted March 3, 1931.*

State Bird

Yellowhammer — *Named for the color beneath its wings, the yellowhammer is a kind of woodpecker. Due to the color of their uniforms, Alabama's Confederate soldiers were often referred to as "yellowhammers." Alabama is also called the "Yellowhammer State."*

State Game Bird

Wild turkey — *Today Alabama has one of the nation's largest per-acre wild turkey populations.*

State Saltwater Fish

Fighting tarpon — *Found off the coast of Alabama, this fish can weigh as much as 100 pounds (45 kilograms).*

State Reptile

Alabama red-bellied turtle — *Found only in Alabama, the Alabama red-bellied turtle has yellow stripes on its legs, neck, and head and reaches up to 13 inches (33 centimeters) in length.*

State Insect

Monarch butterfly

State Tree

Southern longleaf pine

State Flower

Camellia

State Nut

Pecan

State Mineral

Hematite — *This red iron ore helped establish Birmingham as an industrial powerhouse.*

State Shell

Johnstone's junonia — *This shell is named after Kathleen Yerger Johnstone, an amateur seashell expert.*

State Amphibian

Red Hills salamander

PLACES TO VISIT

Ivy Green, *Tuscumbia*
Ivy Green is the birthplace of Helen Keller, a social reformer and advocate for disabled people. Keller's home is on the National Register of Historic Places and is open to the public.

Alabama Jazz Hall of Fame, *Birmingham*
Alabama's many talented jazz musicians are honored in this museum, which is housed in the Carver Theatre for the Performing Arts.

U.S. Space & Rocket Center, *Huntsville*
A trip to Huntsville's Tranquillity Base brings you to the U.S. Space & Rocket Center. This center has hands-on astronaut training exhibits and a large collection of spacecrafts and rockets.

Russell Cave National Monument, *near Bridgeport*
At this site archaeologists have discovered tools and artifacts of prehistoric peoples who inhabited the cave as early as 7000 B.C.

For other places and events, see p. 44.

BIGGEST, BEST, AND MOST

- Alabama is the only state that possesses all the raw materials necessary for the production of iron and steel.

- The likeness of the Roman god Vulcan that overlooks Birmingham from nearby Red Mountain is the largest cast-iron statue in the world.

- Alabama introduced the Mardi Gras celebration to the Western Hemisphere.

STATE FIRSTS

- **1909** The Wrights start the nation's first flight school in Montgomery.
- **1972** Johnny Ford is elected mayor of Tuskegee, making him the first African-American mayor in Alabama's history. He served six terms.
- **1992** Dr. Mae Jemison becomes the first African-American woman to fly in space.

The Tuskegee Airmen

During World War II, the U.S. armed forces were still segregated — African Americans trained and fought in separate units. No program existed for training African-American military pilots until activists and newspapers pressured the government to create one. In 1941, the 99th Pursuit Squadron, an African-American unit, was formed. These soldiers received their flight training at the Tuskegee Institute, an African-American college in Alabama. After more than two years of training, the Tuskegee Airmen, as they came to be known, flew the first of many combat missions off the coast of Italy. Nearly one thousand African-American men completed flight training by the war's end in 1945. The distinguished service of the Tuskegee Airmen, who collectively won 850 medals, helped bring about the 1948 desegregation of the U.S. armed services.

Unclaimed Luggage

In Scottsboro, a store called Unclaimed Baggage sells a variety of goods at reasonable prices. Most of the items — including clothing, cameras, jewelry, and, of course, luggage — are from airline baggage never claimed by their owners or personal items passengers left on airplanes. The airlines spend at least two months trying to track down the owners. When no owner can be found, these items make their way to Unclaimed Baggage to be sold at bargain prices.

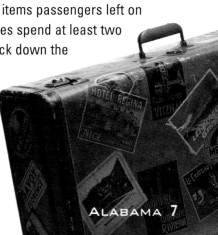

Old Traditions, New Horizons

> A clang of sabres mid Virginian snow,
> The fiery pang of shells,—
> And there's a wail of immemorial woe
> In Alabama dells.
>
> — *from "John Pelham," a poem by James Ryder Randall,*
> *in* An American Anthology, *1900.*

Humans first came to the region we now call Alabama as early as twelve thousand years ago. These Paleo-Indians were nomadic hunter-gatherers who used Alabama's extensive network of caves for shelter. Archaeologists have discovered traces of their tools and other artifacts in such places as Russell Cave in northeastern Jackson County and the Stanfield-Worley bluff shelter in Colbert County. By about 7000 B.C., Alabama's earliest residents had abandoned their rocky homes in favor of temporary shelters made from animal skins. They had organized themselves into tribal units by A.D. 700 and practiced agriculture in permanent settlements. By the time Europeans began exploring Alabama, Native American tribes such as the Alabama, Cherokee, Creek, Choctaw, and Chickasaw inhabited the region.

Native Americans of Alabama
Alabama
Cherokee
Chickasaw
Choctaw
Creek

European Exploration

Nearly five centuries ago Europeans began to explore and map the Alabama region. In 1507, German mapmaker Martin Waldseemüller mapped the outline of Mobile Bay, based in part on information collected during the voyages of the Italian explorer Amerigo Vespucci, after whom the Americas are named. The first known European explorer to see Alabama close-up was Spaniard Alonso Alvarez de Piñeda, who sailed into Mobile Bay in 1519. A succession of Spanish explorers passed through the region in later years, including Pánfilo de Narváez in 1528. It was Spaniard Hernando de Soto, however, who first explored the region extensively, looking for gold. Another Spaniard, adventurer Tristán de Luna, arrived in Alabama in 1559, also in search

DID YOU KNOW?

The Alabama (or Alibamu) were a Native American tribe inhabiting the region that came to have their name. There is some disagreement among scholars on the precise meaning of the name. Today, *Alabama* is popularly translated as "to open [or clear] the thicket."

of gold. In the process he established the first European settlements in the area around Mobile Bay (near present-day Claiborne). Stormy weather and lack of food led to great hardships, and these settlements were abandoned by 1561.

Although the Spanish were Alabama's earliest European explorers, the French established the region's first permanent European settlements. Two French-Canadian brothers — Pierre Le Moyne, Sieur d'Iberville, and Jean Baptiste Le Moyne, Sieur de Bienville — reached Mobile Bay in 1699. In 1702, they founded Fort Louis de la Mobile along the Mobile River. In 1711, floods caused this settlement to be moved to the site of present-day Mobile. It served as the capital of French Louisiana until 1718 and was renamed Fort Conde in 1720. The French established several other forts in the region, including Fort Tombecbé near the Tombigbee and Black Warrior Rivers in 1736.

The French and Indian War

During this period of French settlement, English traders and settlers began moving into northern Alabama. Tensions over territory in North America, as well as in Europe, caused the French and English to battle one another sporadically. Tensions grew and led to what became known as the French and Indian War, which was fought from 1754 to 1763. At the end of the war, the French turned their territories east of the Mississippi River, with the exception of New Orleans, over to

City of Gold

De Soto's exploration of southeastern North America was driven by a search for gold. His ill treatment of the Native Americans he encountered caused them to tell him what he wanted to hear — that there was a land of gold to be found, but it lay elsewhere. De Soto never found a city of gold, but his exploration of the continent was the first step toward European settlement and, eventually, the establishment of Alabama, Florida, and other states.

▼ The French and Indian War began in Alabama over territorial disputes between French trappers and English settlers.

Great Britain. What is now northern Alabama was incorporated into the Illinois Country, while the region around Mobile became part of British West Florida.

The British then came into conflict with the Spanish who held Florida. Spain declared war on Great Britain in 1779 while the British were fighting the Revolutionary War and attempting to subdue their thirteen rebellious North American colonies. Bernardo de Galvez of Spain took control of Mobile from the British in 1780. At the end of the Revolutionary War in 1783, the British signed a treaty that recognized the new United States and turned the Mobile region over to Spain. The northern and central areas of present-day Alabama, claimed by the state of Georgia, were under U.S. control. The United States and Spain, however, did not agree on the boundary between Georgia and Spanish-controlled Florida, thus creating considerable tension between the two countries.

Indian Wars and the Alabama Territory

The border dispute was settled when U.S. statesman Thomas Pinckney negotiated the Treaty of San Lorenzo with Spain in 1795. The treaty established new boundaries, which made all of what is now Alabama — except for the Mobile region that remained under Spanish control — part of the United States. The U.S. Congress incorporated this region into the Mississippi Territory in 1798. Then, on April 15, 1813, troops under the command of U.S. General James Wilkinson wrested control of the Mobile area from Spain. The entire Alabama region was finally under the control of the United States.

The U.S. government faced a difficult situation as relations between Native Americans and non-Native settlers grew increasingly hostile and fighting began. In 1811, Shawnee chief Tecumseh rallied the region's Native peoples to join other Native Americans in opposing the settlers. Native Americans in what is now Alabama did resist the influx of white settlers, sometimes using violence, but their victories were short-lived. In March 1814, General Andrew Jackson led U.S. troops into battle against Creek warriors led by William Weatherford, also known as Red Eagle. After the U.S. victory at the Battle of Horseshoe Bend, Creek lands were seized. In 1817 the U.S. Congress organized the Alabama Territory, making St. Stephens on the Tombigbee River its capital. As white settlement increased, the Creek, Cherokee, and Choctaw living in Alabama were forced to move west. In the 1830s, the U.S. government forced most Native Americans in the region to give up their land and resettle in what is now Oklahoma.

Statehood

In 1819, Huntsville was the site of a convention that produced the Alabama Territory's first constitution. Alabama became the twenty-second state of the Union on December 14, 1819, with Huntsville serving as Alabama's capital for slightly more than a year. William Wyatt Bibb became Alabama's first state governor. The state capital was moved to Cahaba in 1820. Due to severe flooding, the capital was moved once again in 1826, this time to Tuscaloosa.

Secession and the Civil War

In the 1840s, a political movement advocating abolition (the prohibition of slavery) gained momentum in the United States, particularly in the northern states. Abolitionists petitioned the federal government to bar slavery in the western territories and anywhere else it was practiced within the nation. A state convention of the Democratic party met in 1848 to address this issue. Party members there adopted William L. Yancey's "Alabama Platform," which stated that the federal government had no right to outlaw slavery in the territories.

Arguments over slavery raged throughout the 1850s, driving a wedge between the slave states of the South and the free states of the North. The election of Abraham Lincoln as the U.S. president brought these conflicts to a boil, and, on January 11, 1861, Alabama seceded

Tecumseh

Tecumseh (1768–1813) was a warrior-chief of the Shawnee people. With his brother Tenskwatawa, he worked to halt the expansion of white settlement in the Northwest Territory. Tecumseh struggled to unify rival Native peoples to prevent the sale of Native American lands to the United States. After the tribes in the Indiana Territory gave up large tracts of land to the United States in 1809, Tecumseh protested to Indiana territorial governor William Henry Harrison. He argued, without success, that all Native peoples owned these lands as common property. Despite his failure to invalidate this land transaction, Tecumseh continued his work to unite Native peoples. In late 1811, he traveled to Alabama and other regions to build a coalition among the Chickasaw, Choctaw, and Creek peoples. While Tecumseh had some success in his travels, his brother launched an offensive against U.S. troops. With Tenskwatawa's defeat in the Battle of Tippecanoe, Tecumseh's coalition was mostly destroyed. Tecumseh did not give up the fight, however. He brought two thousand warriors into the War of 1812 on the side of the British. He died a warrior's death on October 5, 1813, while leading his men into the Battle of the Thames at Chatham, Ontario, in Canada.

(withdrew) from the Union, renaming itself the Republic of Alabama.

Alabama invited other Southern states to send delegates to its secession convention. Delegates from seven Southern states met in Montgomery on February 4, 1861, to organize themselves into a new, separate nation. Four days later the convention established the Confederate States of America. Montgomery, known as "the Cradle of the Confederacy," served as its capital until May 1861, when the capital was moved to Richmond, Virginia.

Union and Confederate forces clashed at Fort Sumter, South Carolina, in April 1861, starting the Civil War. Alabama was the site of many Civil War battles. One of the most important was the Battle of Mobile Bay. On August 5, 1864, Rear Admiral David G. Farragut defeated Confederate forces and blockaded the bay. This victory led to the capture of the city of Mobile and then to a general Union occupation of Alabama by April 1865. Cities such as Montgomery and Selma were partially destroyed by Union forces during the war, although much of Alabama emerged from the conflict largely unscathed.

Reconstruction and Reform

The period known as Reconstruction followed the Confederacy's surrender in 1865. During this time the federal government attempted to repair the damage done by the war and to integrate the Southern states into the Union. Alabama, like all former Confederate states, had to guarantee the civil rights of African Americans before it was readmitted to the Union in 1868. A coalition of African

Full Speed Ahead!

Rear Admiral David G. Farragut was responsible for one of the most decisive Union victories of the Civil War. In 1864, Farragut led a fleet of eighteen ships (*left*) into Mobile Bay to cut off Confederate supplies of munitions and other much-needed goods. A small Confederate fleet stood against Farragut's forces and torpedoed the admiral's flagship, the U.S.S. *Tecumseh*. Unfazed, Farragut drove his remaining ships forward to capture Mobile Bay, which led to the Union occupation of all of Alabama the following year.

Americans and their Northern and pro-Union Southern allies controlled the state government for most of the next six years. These Republicans attempted to restore the economy and improve the state's transportation network as well as promote the education and civil rights of African Americans. Alabama's Reconstruction period ended in 1874, however. Conservative Democrats, who opposed the rights granted to African Americans, were elected to most state offices. These new officials reorganized the state's massive debt and wrote a new state constitution, which was adopted in 1875. In theory, this constitution protected certain African-American civil rights, such as voting and property rights. In practice, Alabama's African-American citizens were subject to the segregationist "Jim Crow" laws, which stripped them of their newly won rights and prevented them from sharing public facilities with whites. As late as the 1960s, these laws routinely prevented African Americans from exercising basic constitutional rights.

The Twentieth Century

By the beginning of the new century, Alabama's economy had recovered from the devastation of the Civil War. The state became a center for the iron, steel, and textile industries. When the United States entered World War I, about seventy-four thousand Alabamians entered the armed forces and helped win the war. World War I greatly spurred economic growth in Alabama. Demand increased significantly for cotton and food crops from the state's many farms. The Alabama State Docks agency opened new port facilities at Mobile by the mid-1920s, increasing the state's participation in international trade.

This new prosperity was not destined to last long. Alabama suffered along with every other state in the Union when the stock market crashed in 1929. The crash unleashed economic depression and high unemployment. The Great Depression led to financial panic in Alabama when more than sixty of the state's banks failed between 1929 and

Blight or Blessing?

In 1915, Alabama's agricultural economy suffered an almost killing blow with the arrival of an insect called the boll weevil. This destructive pest wiped out most of Alabama's all-important cotton crop and forced farmers all over Alabama to switch to other crops or raise livestock. Although hard-hit by the boll weevil scourge, residents of Enterprise, a town in southeastern Alabama, were later grateful for the disaster. The crops that replaced cotton — corn, peanuts, and soybeans — proved more valuable. Today, the town of Enterprise is the site of a public monument to the insatiable boll weevil, which proved to be a blessing in disguise.

1931. To make matters worse, flooding in the Alabama–Tombigbee River system caused about $6 million in damage in 1929. With the state government facing imminent bankruptcy, Alabama passed its first state income tax law in an effort to stay afloat financially.

The federal government helped turn the fiscal tide for Alabama — and several other struggling states — when it created the Tennessee Valley Authority (TVA) in 1933. The TVA built flood-control systems and electrical power-generation facilities along the Tennessee River, providing much-needed jobs and improving the quality of life for people in the region. Private industry also rallied to help Alabama's economic recovery, with the Alabama Power Company building several hydroelectric plants. The inexpensive electrical power these plants produced helped keep Alabama's factories running — and played a part in pulling the state out of the Great Depression.

World War II and the Postwar Years

The United States's involvement in World War II, which began in 1941, greatly stimulated Alabama's agricultural and industrial productivity. In 1941, the federal government established Huntsville's Redstone Arsenal, where many of the rockets and spacecrafts used by the U.S. space program were later developed. Following the war, Alabama's manufacturing sector focused on the production of chemicals, rubber

▼ In 1969, Neil Armstrong and Edwin "Buzz" Aldrin planted the U.S. flag on the Moon. The astronauts arrived with the help of the *Saturn V* rocket, which was constructed in Alabama.

products, textiles, and minerals.

The state economy slowed considerably during the 1950s. This slowdown prompted many Alabamians to seek work in other states. New technology on farms reduced the need for human labor, forcing many farm laborers to seek work in the cities, and Alabama became an increasingly urban state. In 1960, the federal government opened the George C. Marshall Space Flight Center at Huntsville. The powerful *Saturn V* rocket, which carried U.S. astronauts to the Moon between 1968 and 1972, was developed there.

Winds of Change

In 1954, a U.S. Supreme Court decision declared public school segregation unconstitutional. Alabama race relations remained tense as African Americans took increasingly strong stands against injustice. In 1955, the arrest of Rosa Parks sparked civil rights actions across Alabama. Dr. Martin Luther King, Jr., a civil rights leader and minister, led a boycott of the bus system, prompting a federal court to order the system to desegregate. Governor George C. Wallace continued to oppose integration of the state's schools as late as 1963, and the federal government had to call out the National Guard to ensure integration. When the U.S. Congress passed the Civil Rights Act of 1964, Alabama had to desegregate its public facilities, such as restaurants, rest rooms, and drinking fountains.

In March 1965, Dr. King led a march from Selma to Montgomery to protest discrimination against African-American voters. This action, among others, led the U.S. Congress to pass the Voting Rights Act (1965), which enabled thousands of African-American Alabamians to register to vote. Civil rights events in Alabama transformed race relations in U.S. society as a whole. Today, race relations in the state are much improved, although battles continue over who should control the fate of the region and what shape the future should take.

The Quiet Rebellion

Rosa Louise McCauley Parks (1913–) was a key figure in the Civil Rights Movement. Parks's refusal to yield her bus seat to a white passenger — as mandated by Alabama's segregation laws — touched off the 1955–1956 Montgomery bus boycott. At that time, Parks was the secretary for the local branch of the National Association for the Advancement of Colored People (NAACP), a reflection of her lifelong commitment to civil rights.

Parks's courageous stand resulted in the loss of her job as a seamstress and housekeeper, but her bold actions placed public officials on notice that discrimination would not be tolerated and inspired others to challenge the unjust treatment of African Americans during the 1950s. Parks was awarded the Congressional Gold Medal of Honor in 1999.

A State Moving Forward

> While over Alabama earth
> These words are gently spoken:
> Serve — and hate will die unborn.
> Love — and chains are broken.
>
> — *Langston Hughes, U.S. poet, "Alabama Earth
> (at Booker Washington's grave)," Golden Slippers (1941)*

Alabama's population, totaling 4,447,100 according to the 2000 census, ranks it as the twenty-third most populous state in the Union. Alabama's growth has accelerated in the last decade. Between 1990 and 2000 the population grew by more than 10 percent; in the 1980s, it experienced an increase of only 4.5 percent. Alabama's increasing population reflects the state's continued industrial growth and its hopeful prospects for the future.

A History of Growth
When the U.S. Congress declared Alabama a territory in 1817, settlers rushed in to claim parcels of the area's fertile farmland. Within two years, the Alabama Territory's population had grown enough to qualify the region for

Age Distribution in Alabama
(2000 Census)

0–4	295,992
5–19	960,177
20–24	306,865
25–44	1,288,527
45–64	1,015,741
65 & over	579,798

Across One Hundred Years
Alabama's three largest foreign-born groups for 1890 and 1990

1890 — Germany 3,945; England 2,934; Ireland 2,604
Total state population: 1,513,017
Total foreign-born: 14,776 (1%)

1990 — Germany 5,685; United Kingdom 3,348; Canada 2,477
Total state population: 4,040,587
Total foreign-born: 43,533 (1%)

Patterns of Immigration
The total number of people who immigrated to Alabama in 1998 was 1,608. Of that number, the largest immigrant groups were from Mexico (11.1%), India (10.3%), and the People's Republic of China (7.3%).

statehood, which — along with the forced removal of Alabama's Native peoples — ushered in still more waves of settlers from other states and nations.

During the decade following Alabama's entry into the Union, new settlers doubled the state's free and slave populations. The system of slavery was essential for maintaining Alabama's primarily cotton-based economy. In 1860, right before the outbreak of the Civil War, Alabama's booming cotton plantations were supporting a population of 964,201 people; 55 percent were white while 45 percent — the vast majority of whom were slaves — were African American. From the end of the Civil War into the mid-1900s, many African Americans became sharecroppers. Sharecroppers worked another person's land in exchange for a share in the profits. Landlords used this system to exploit the poor, both black and white, squeezing the tenants for every penny they earned and often driving them into debt by overcharging for supplies and other necessities. In the 1880s and 1890s, large numbers of western European immigrants settled in Alabama, and many found work in the Birmingham area's mines and steel foundries.

▲ Cotton fields grow around the home of African-American sharecroppers, circa 1937.

Heritage and Background, Alabama | Year 2000

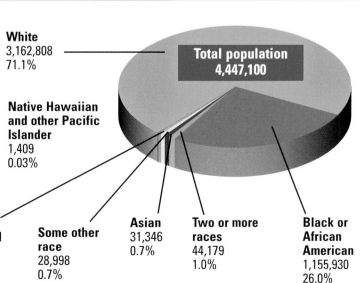

▶ Here's a look at the racial backgrounds of Alabamians today. Alabama ranks seventh among all U.S. states with regard to African Americans as a percentage of the population.

White
3,162,808
71.1%

Total population
4,447,100

Native Hawaiian and other Pacific Islander
1,409
0.03%

American Indian and Alaska Native
22,430
0.5%

Some other race
28,998
0.7%

Asian
31,346
0.7%

Two or more races
44,179
1.0%

Black or African American
1,155,930
26.0%

Note: 17% (75,830) of the population identify themselves as **Hispanic** or **Latino,** a cultural designation that crosses racial lines. Hispanics and Latinos are counted in this category as well as the racial category of their choice.

The growth rate of the state's population slowed during the mid-twentieth century. This slow growth was due in part to the departure of many African Americans who left the state in search of better social and economic climates in northern states. Since the late 1980s, Alabama's population has continued to grow, although this increase has included few immigrants. In 1990, only 1 percent of Alabama's population was foreign-born.

Where Do Alabamians Live?

About 60 percent of Alabama's residents live in such metropolitan areas as Anniston, Birmingham, Huntsville, Mobile, Montgomery, and Tuscaloosa. During the 1950s, the population of Huntsville grew by 340 percent as thousands settled in the area to work at the U.S. Army's Redstone Arsenal and, later, the George C. Marshall Space Flight Center. Birmingham remains Alabama's most populous city.

Education

As the nineteenth-century, cotton-plantation economy brought prosperity to Alabama's landed elite, schools and colleges were established, newspapers began publication, and stately public and private buildings were erected.

▼ The city of Birmingham was founded in 1813 and is now one of the state's major metropolitan areas.

Alabama suffered from an overall lack of educational resources, however, until 1854. In that year, Alabama established a statewide public school system.

Like most southern states, Alabama had a policy of segregation, meaning that African-American and white students were sent to separate schools. In the U.S. Supreme Court decision *Brown v. Board of Education of Topeka, Kansas* (1954), the practice was ruled unconstitutional. Alabama was slow to embrace this change because of entrenched racism and did not begin desegregating its public schools until 1963. Ten years later large-scale school integration had finally been achieved. During the 1980s a bond initiative greatly benefited the state's public schools. Today the state boasts a total of about 46,000 elementary and secondary school teachers.

Nearly eighty institutions of higher learning operate within Alabama, including the University of Alabama system, established in 1831, with campuses at Tuscaloosa, Birmingham, and Huntsville. Other important colleges and universities include Auburn University (with the largest student population in the state), Jacksonville State University, Samford University, and Tuskegee University.

Religion

Alabama lies near the heart of a region often referred to as the "Bible Belt." The majority of Alabamians (at 67.7 percent of the population) belong to various Protestant Christian denominations. Over half are Baptists. Other Protestant denominations in Alabama include United Methodists, Presbyterians, Episcopalians, and Evangelical Lutherans. Just 3 percent of Alabamians are Roman Catholic. The state is also home to small numbers of Jews, Muslims, and Hindus.

Believe in Alabama

Religious beliefs can sometimes lead to political action. When Dr. Martin Luther King, Jr., a Baptist minister, condemned racism from the pulpit, he helped bring about the Civil Rights Movement in the 1950s and 1960s. In more recent decades, debates over freedom of religious expression have raged in the state. In 1997, when a federal court ordered an Alabama county judge to refrain from leading prayers in his courtroom, religious Alabamians took to the streets of Montgomery to express their displeasure. Alabama's supreme court dismissed the case the following year, giving at least a temporary victory to the judge and his supporters. Religion, in its many forms, continues to shape the lives of many Alabamians.

Educational Levels of Alabama Workers (age 25 and over)	
Less than 9th grade	348,848
9th to 12th grade, no diploma	494,790
High school graduate, including equivalency	749,591
Some college, no degree or associate degree	553,512
Bachelor's degree	258,231
Graduate or professional degree	140,997

A Country of Vast Resources

> Alabama, your beautiful highways
> Are carved through the mountains
> Where loved ones do wait.
> Alabama, your goldenrod flowers
> And the "welcome home" sign
> Hanging over the gate.
>
> — *from the song "Alabama," by country singers Ira and Charlie Louvin*

From the mountains in the north to the beaches in the south, Alabama's landscape is nothing if not varied. Between the mountains and beaches lie lakes, hills, forests, and prime farmland. Throughout the state, rivers form a transportation network and generate hydroelectric power. Mineral deposits such as coal, iron ore, limestone, and marble are significant economic assets. Natural attractions such as DeSoto Falls, Natural Bridge, and the many caverns in northern Alabama make spectacular destinations for hikers and tourists.

Region by Region

Northern Alabama features hills and pine forests as well as the southernmost ranges of the Appalachian Mountains. The Tennessee River Valley in the northwestern corner of the state offers water transportation routes and hydroelectric power to support manufacturing centers in Decatur, Florence, Muscle Shoals, Sheffield, and Tuscumbia. Northeastern

Highest Point
Cheaha Mountain
2,407 feet (734 m)
above sea level

▼ *From left to right:* the white, sandy beaches of Alabama's Gulf Coast; a view of Little River Canyon; DeSoto Falls; flowers at the Birmingham Botanical Gardens; a view from the bottom of a 160-foot (49-m) cavern; Alabama opossums.

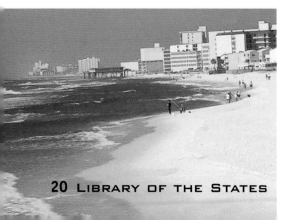

Alabama is part of the Appalachian Plateau, which rises to an elevation of about 1,800 feet (549 m). Here, on the relatively flat land, farmers grow cotton, hay, and potatoes and raise hogs and poultry. In general, flat plains, rolling hills, and deep, river-formed ravines characterize western Alabama.

The terrain in the southern two-thirds of the state is mainly flat, covered by farms and pine forests. This region is home to Alabama's prime agricultural land, including parts of the Black Belt zone, so named because of its dark clay soil. Exceptions to the otherwise flat region are the hills and ridges of east-central Alabama. They contain abundant reserves of iron ore, coal, marble, and limestone. Manufacturers in this region use hydroelectric power generated on the Coosa and Tallapoosa Rivers.

In the extreme southwest, there are vast stretches of swamp, marsh, and bayou, beyond which lie the beaches of Mobile Bay and the Gulf Shore. Alabama boasts 53 miles (85 km) of sandy coastline along the Gulf of Mexico. Including its many small inlets, this shoreline runs a length of 607 miles (977 km). Mobile Bay is Alabama's gateway to the Gulf of Mexico and the world, in terms of international shipping. Alabama's coastline is also home to Perdido Bay, which offers beaches, recreational facilities, and historic sites. Near Mobile Bay, the freshwater of the Mobile and Tensaw Rivers mixes with saltwater from the Gulf to form estuaries — unique habitats for marine life. Alabama's estuaries have suffered from industrial pollution, but, in 1995, the state government committed itself to protecting these fragile ecosystems by entering the National Estuary Program cleanup project.

Lakes and Rivers

Alabama is blessed with large amounts of freshwater, thanks in part to the Tennessee River and its artificial lakes. These lakes and their dams provide drinking water

Average January temperature
Mobile: 50°F (10°C)
Birmingham: 43°F (6°C)

Average July temperature
Mobile: 82°F (28°C)
Birmingham: 80°F (27°C)

Average yearly rainfall
Mobile: 67 inches (170.2 cm)
Birmingham: 53 inches (134.6 cm)

Average yearly snowfall
Mobile: 0.4 inch (1 cm)
Birmingham: 1.2 inches (3 cm)

Major Rivers

Tennessee River
650 miles (1,046 km)

Chattahoochee River
410 miles (660 km)

Alabama River
315 miles (507 km)

Tombigbee River
300 miles (483 km)

Coosa River
286 miles (460 km)

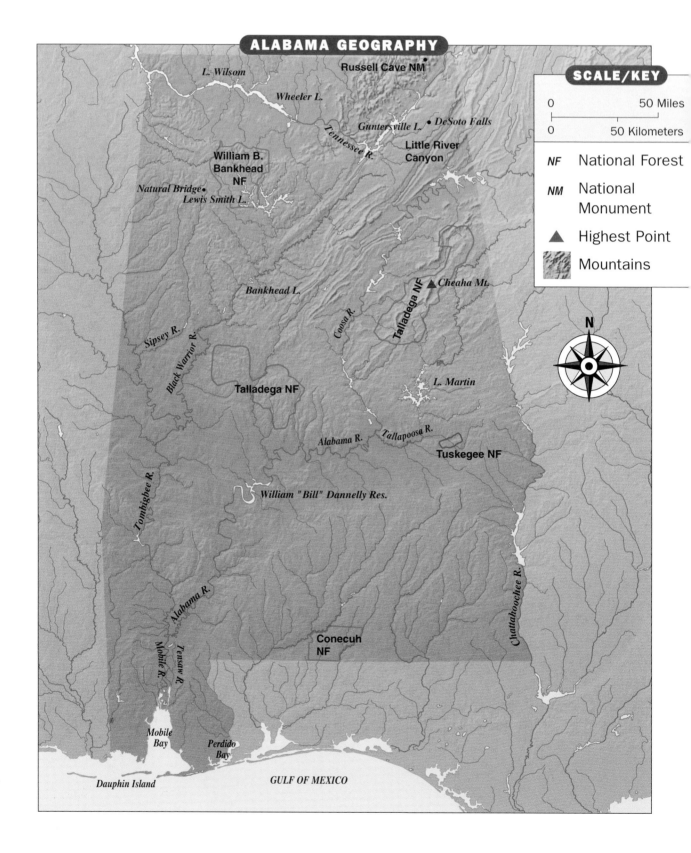

ALABAMA GEOGRAPHY

L. Wilsom

Russell Cave NM

Wheeler L.

Guntersville L.
DeSoto Falls

Tennessee R.

Little River
Canyon

William B.
Bankhead
NF

Natural Bridge
Lewis Smith L.

Bankhead L.

Sipsey R.

Black Warrior R.

Coosa R.

Talladega NF

Cheaha Mt.

Talladega NF

L. Martin

Alabama R.

Tallapoosa R.

Tuskegee NF

Tombigbee R.

William "Bill" Dannelly Res.

Chattahoochee R.

Alabama R.

Conecuh
NF

Mobile R.

Tensaw R.

Mobile
Bay

Perdido
Bay

Dauphin Island

GULF OF MEXICO

SCALE/KEY

0 — 50 Miles

0 — 50 Kilometers

NF — National Forest

NM — National Monument

▲ — Highest Point

Mountains

N

and recreation, and they also generate hydroelectric power. The Tombigbee and Alabama Rivers flow southward and meet to form the Mobile River before emptying into the Gulf of Mexico.

Climate

Alabama's climate ranges from temperate in the north to subtropical in the south. Summers are hot, humid, and rainy. Southern Alabama receives the majority of the yearly overall precipitation. Sometimes this precipitation falls during late-summer hurricanes. Tornadoes appear most frequently during March and April.

Plants and Animals

Much of Alabama is densely forested. Various pines, hickories, and oaks dominate in the northern forests. During the spring, Alabama's countryside comes alive with camellias, hydrangeas, and many other kinds of plant life. The estuaries near Mobile Bay support plants that have adapted to a saltwater environment.

Alabama's diverse animal population includes black bears, bobcats, opossums, and wild turkeys. Alabama's lowland swamps support dam-building beavers, while alligators can be found in the swamps, bayous, and estuaries of southern Alabama.

Largest Lakes

Guntersville Lake
69,100 acres (27,965 ha)

Wheeler Lake
68,300 acres (27,641 ha)

Lake Martin
39,000 acres (15,783 ha)

▼ Lake Guntersville State Park has 5,909 acres (2,391 ha) of wilderness surrounding Guntersville Lake.

Alabama's Worthy Labors

> Each is under the most sacred obligation not to squander the material committed to him, not to sap his strength in folly and vice, and to see at the least that he delivers a product worthy the labor and cost which have been expended on him.
>
> — *Anna Julia Cooper (c.1859–1964), African-American educator and feminist,* A Voice from the South, *part 2 (1892).*

By the time Alabama was admitted to the Union in 1819, settlers were busy clearing wilderness for farms and building towns in Alabama's river valleys. As the nineteenth century progressed, farmers began to rely increasingly on cotton as a "cash crop." The plantation economy that developed brought prosperity to Alabama's major landholders, especially in the fertile plains known as the Black Belt that extend through central Alabama.

Rough Times and Recovery

In the late nineteenth century, several railroad lines were built in Alabama, and iron and steel manufacturing began. Alabama's abundant deposits of coal, iron ore, and limestone — the three substances required to produce iron and steel — enabled the state to become an industry leader. In addition to steel and iron, the textile and lumber industries also expanded.

Farmers, however, experienced tough times. Many were sharecroppers who labored under harsh economic conditions. To address the plight of Alabama's farmers, reform groups such as the Farmers' Alliance and the Populists tried to elect state agricultural commissioner Reuben F. Kolb to the governorship in the 1890, 1892, and 1894 elections. Although Kolb's candidacy failed each time, many of the reformers' demands eventually became law.

"King Cotton" ruled Alabama's rural economy until 1915, when an infestation of insects known as boll weevils caused the state's cotton crop to fail. Compounded by yearly

Top Employers
(of workers age sixteen and over)

Services	29.4%
Manufacturing	22.9%
Wholesale and retail trade	20.3%
Construction	7.1%
Transportation, communications, and public utilities	7.0%
Public Administration	5.3%
Finance, insurance, and real estate	5.0%
Agriculture, forestry, and fisheries	2.3%
Mining	0.7%

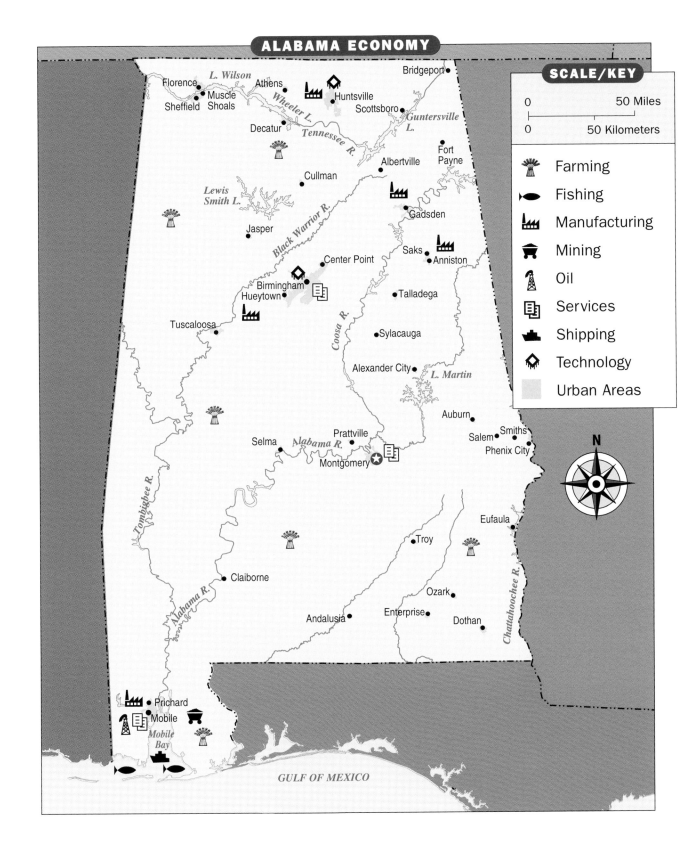

ALABAMA ECONOMY

SCALE/KEY

0	50 Miles
0	50 Kilometers

- Farming
- Fishing
- Manufacturing
- Mining
- Oil
- Services
- Shipping
- Technology
- Urban Areas

Florence
L. Wilson
Athens
Bridgeport
Muscle Shoals
Sheffield
Wheeler L.
Huntsville
Scottsboro
Guntersville L.
Decatur
Tennessee R.
Fort Payne
Albertville
Cullman
Lewis Smith L.
Gadsden
Jasper
Black Warrior R.
Saks
Anniston
Center Point
Birmingham
Hueytown
Talladega
Coosa R.
Tuscaloosa
Sylacauga
Alexander City
L. Martin
Auburn
Selma
Alabama R.
Prattville
Salem
Smiths
Phenix City
Montgomery
Tombigbee R.
Eufaula
Troy
Claiborne
Alabama R.
Ozark
Andalusia
Enterprise
Dothan
Chattahoochee R.

N

Prichard
Mobile
Mobile Bay
GULF OF MEXICO

fluctuations in the price of cotton, this catastrophe forced Alabama's farmers to grow a variety of crops. Bitter experience proved that dependence on a single crop could be costly and devastating. Although cotton remains the number one crop today, Alabama farmers have diversified and also raise cattle and poultry and grow corn, peanuts, and soybeans.

Modern Alabama

At the outset of the twenty-first century, manufacturing makes up about one-fourth of Alabama's gross state product (the total value of all goods produced and services provided). Anniston, Birmingham, Gadsden, Huntsville, and Mobile are among Alabama's most important manufacturing centers.

Thanks to Alabama's well-developed transportation network, the output of Alabama's manufacturing cities can make its way around the world. The Tennessee–Tombigbee Waterway, completed in 1985, connects northeastern Mississippi to the Mobile seaport.

Service industries employ more Alabamians than any other sector. The sale of products to both businesses and consumers is one of Alabama's most important service industries. The state and federal governments are also large employers in Alabama. Government employees include office workers, schoolteachers, and military personnel, among others.

While vital to the economy, agriculture uses only about 30 percent of the state's land area and employs around 2 percent of the workforce; 41,000 farms are currently

Made in Alabama

Leading farm products and crops
Cotton
Soybeans
Peanuts
Poultry products
Cattle

Other products
Electronics
Cast iron and plastic pipe
Fabricated steel
Ships
Paper products
Chemicals
Steel
Mobile homes
Fabrics

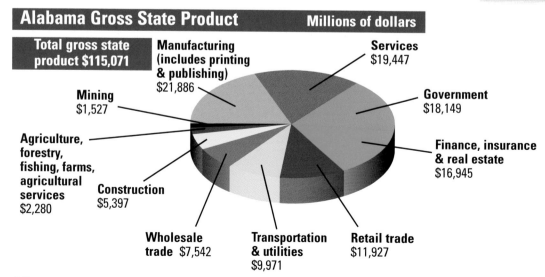

Alabama Gross State Product — Millions of dollars

Total gross state product $115,071

Manufacturing (includes printing & publishing) $21,886

Services $19,447

Government $18,149

Finance, insurance & real estate $16,945

Mining $1,527

Agriculture, forestry, fishing, farms, agricultural services $2,280

Construction $5,397

Wholesale trade $7,542

Transportation & utilities $9,971

Retail trade $11,927

operating in Alabama. Livestock, including poultry and cattle, accounts for about 75 percent of Alabama's farm income. Soybeans, cotton, and peanuts are some leading crops. Alabama's extensive pine forests provide the nation with lumber and pulpwood. The Gulf of Mexico provides catches of shrimp, oysters, croakers, red snapper, and catfish for Alabama's fishing industry. Among the minerals extracted by Alabama's mining concerns are bauxite (aluminum ore), petroleum, natural gas, bituminous coal, clay, and marble.

With the popularity of beach resorts along Alabama's Gulf Coast, tourism contributes significantly to the state's economy. Alabama's extensive national forests, state parks, and rivers attract large numbers of recreational hunters and fishers each year. The state's many historic landmarks are also popular tourist destinations.

Recent Problems — and Solutions

Alabama has rebounded from the economic hardships of the 1980s and early 1990s. The ongoing development of Internet-related commerce has spurred renewed economic growth and attracted new workers to the state. The search for alternatives to dependence on foreign oil as fuel may benefit the Alabama coal industry. Today, Alabama's workers, government officials, and business leaders are looking forward to a bright future.

▼ Passenger planes at Huntsville International Airport. Huntsville is Alabama's second-busiest airport.

Major Airports

Airport	Location	Passengers per year (2000)
Birmingham International	Birmingham	3,067,777
Huntsville International	Huntsville	1,098,740
Mobile Regional	Mobile	784,212

The Privileges of the Law

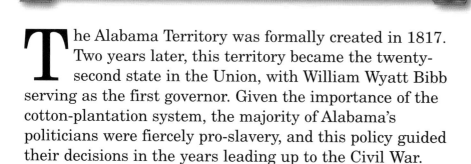

> It is important and right that all privileges of the law be ours, but it is vastly more important that we be prepared for the exercise of those privileges.
>
> — *George Washington Carver, African-American educator and agricultural researcher*

The Alabama Territory was formally created in 1817. Two years later, this territory became the twenty-second state in the Union, with William Wyatt Bibb serving as the first governor. Given the importance of the cotton-plantation system, the majority of Alabama's politicians were fiercely pro-slavery, and this policy guided their decisions in the years leading up to the Civil War.

Leaving and Reentering the Union

Alabama was the fourth Southern state to secede following the 1860 election of Abraham Lincoln to the presidency. When the Civil War was over, Alabama, like the other Confederate states, had to meet certain conditions to reenter the Union. In 1866, Alabama's legislature failed to ratify the Fourteenth Amendment, which guaranteed civil rights for African Americans. The U.S. Congress denied Alabama the right to congressional representation and placed Alabama under military rule in March 1867. The state became part of the Third Military District under the command of General John Pope.

Once the state legislature passed a new state constitution and ratified the Fourteenth Amendment, Alabama rejoined the Union on June 25, 1868. Charges of electoral corruption in the 1890s led to the adoption of another state constitution in 1901, which governs Alabama today.

The Constitution

Alabama's constitution may be amended either by the state legislature or by constitutional convention. Because Alabama's constitution does not allow for "home rule,"

State Constitution

We, the people of the State of Alabama, in order to establish justice, insure domestic tranquillity, and secure the blessings of liberty to ourselves and our posterity, invoking the favor and guidance of Almighty God, do ordain and establish the following Constitution and form of government for the State of Alabama.

— *from Preamble to the 1901 Alabama Constitution*

Elected Posts in the Executive Branch		
Office	Length of Term	Term Limits
Governor	4 years	2 consecutive terms
Lieutenant Governor	4 years	2 consecutive terms
Secretary of State	4 years	2 consecutive terms
Treasurer	4 years	2 consecutive terms
Attorney General	4 years	2 consecutive terms
Commissioner of Labor and Industries	4 years	2 consecutive terms
Superintendent of Public Instruction	4 years	2 consecutive terms

the state's cities and counties can change the way they do business only by means of constitutional amendments. At about 175 times the length of the book in your hands, Alabama's constitution is the longest state constitution in the nation. Because of the constitution's cumbersome size, activists and newspapers around the state began a campaign called the Alabama Constitution Project in the early 1990s. The goal of this ongoing effort is to rewrite and simplify Alabama's constitution.

Executive Branch

Alabama's chief executive officer is the governor, whom the state's voters elect to a four-year term. Although a governor may serve multiple terms, he or she may not serve more than two terms consecutively. The lieutenant governor,

▼ The capitol building in Montgomery was destroyed by fire on December 14, 1849, and was rebuilt on the same site. While additions and improvements have been made over the years, this building still stands today as the home of the Alabama State Legislature.

secretary of state, and attorney general are some of
the other officials who help lead the state government.
Among the governor's most important responsibilities
is the approval or rejection of laws proposed by the state
legislature. The governor is also empowered to grant
criminal pardons and, during times of emergency, may
mobilize the state militia, serving as its commander-in-chief.

Legislative Branch

Alabama has a bicameral, or two-chambered, legislature,
which consists of a 35-member senate and a 105-member
house of representatives. The legislature is responsible for
drafting the state's budget and proposing new laws. The
legislature presents these new laws to the governor, who
may approve or veto them. Alabama's legislators are elected
to four-year terms from the state's 35 senatorial districts
and 105 representative districts.

Judicial Branch

Alabama's highest court is its supreme court. Nine elected
judges serve six-year terms in this court. The head of the
court is the chief justice, and the other eight judges are
known as associate justices. Most criminal and civil cases
are resolved in Alabama's circuit courts, whose decisions
may be challenged in either the court of criminal appeals
or the court of civil appeals. Both of these courts consist
of five judges who each serve a six-year elected term.
Alabama's other courts include district courts, which try
criminal and civil cases, and probate courts, which settle
matters concerning wills and inheritance. Traffic infractions
and other minor issues are handled at the municipal, or
city, court level.

County and Local Governments

County commissions run each of Alabama's sixty-seven
counties. A judge from one of the probate courts typically
runs each commission, serving as chief commissioner for
a six-year term. The sheriff, district attorney, engineer, tax

Mr. King Goes to Washington

William Rufus de Vane King was elected vice president of the United States in 1852. His vice presidency is the highest office in the executive branch of the U.S. government ever achieved by an Alabamian. King took part in the drafting of Alabama's first constitution and served as one of the new state's first U.S. senators. He was an abolitionist and an advocate of peace between the Northern and Southern states. King was asked to be Franklin Pierce's running mate in 1852 to help resolve tensions over the slavery issue in the Democratic party. Unfortunately, tuberculosis took King's life only six weeks after he took office.

State Legislature			
House	Number of Members	Length of Term	Term Limits
Senate	35 senators	4 years	No limits
House of Representatives	105 representatives	4 years	No limits

assessor, tax collector, and superintendent of education are among the other important officials at the county level. Various forms of local government exist in Alabama. A majority of city governments have adopted a mayor-and-city council administration. Birmingham, Huntsville, Montgomery, Tuscaloosa, and most of Alabama's smaller cities employ this system. A few municipalities, however, are governed by a city manager, and others use a commission system modeled after the city manager system that is used on the county level.

Party Politics

The Democratic party dominated national, state, and local politics in Alabama for most of the first half of the twentieth century. Republican and minor-party candidates, however, have grown increasingly influential during the decades following World War II. Presidential candidate Barry M. Goldwater won in Alabama during the 1964 presidential election, becoming the first Republican since 1872 to do so. In 1968, Alabama governor George C. Wallace carried Alabama's electoral votes as the presidential candidate for the American Independent party. Republican presidential candidates have won Alabama's electoral votes consistently since 1980. Recent Alabama governor Guy Hunt (1987–93) became the first Republican to be sworn in as Alabama's chief executive since the early 1870s. Hunt was removed from office in 1993, after being convicted of ethics violations, only to be pardoned in 1998 by a state parole board. Governor Forrest "Fob" James, elected in 1994, was also a Republican.

Democratic and progressive politics are by no means dead in Alabama, however. Running as a Democrat, George C. Wallace was elected to an unprecedented fourth term as Alabama's governor in 1982. The fact that the former segregationist ran on a platform of bettering the lives of all of Alabama's citizens — including the state's African Americans — was a hopeful sign for Alabama's political future. Alabama's current governor, Don Siegelman, is also a Democrat.

From Racism to Redemption

Montgomery-born Democrat George C. Wallace was elected governor of Alabama four times. First elected governor in 1962, he held defiantly segregationist views. In 1963, Wallace tried to keep African-American students from attending the University of Alabama, but he yielded after President John F. Kennedy mobilized the National Guard to enforce the U.S. Supreme Court's desegregation rulings. Wallace was the American Independent party's 1968 presidential candidate; he made another presidential bid in 1972. Wallace was again elected Alabama's governor in 1970 and 1974. On May 15, 1972, Wallace was shot by a would-be assassin and was partially paralyzed. He was elected for a fourth term as Alabama's governor in 1982, this time running on a platform of toleration and respect — a complete reversal of his 1960s-era views. The "politically reborn" George Wallace received significant African-American support. Wallace retired from public life in 1987 and died in 1998.

A Taste for Living

> Jambalaya and a crawfish pie and filet gumbo
> 'Cause tonight I'm gonna meet ma cher amio
> Pick guitar, fill fruit jar, and be gayo
> Son of a gun we'll have big fun on the bayou
>
> *Hank Williams, country music singer and composer,*
> *"Jambalaya," 1952*

The culture of Alabama is the product of a mix of traditions. The Creole people — the descendants of Alabama's earliest non-Native residents — have lent French, Spanish, and African influences to the culture of this Gulf Coast state, from music to literature to cooking to language. Creoles have carefully preserved their cultural heritage, often speaking dialects of either French or Spanish. Although the Creoles are more often associated with Louisiana, their way of life has also profoundly affected Alabama, where Mardi Gras, the celebration that takes place just before the start of the Christian season of Lent, was already a century old before it took root in New Orleans.

Food is central to the Alabama experience, and southern hospitality is one of Alabama's most time-honored traditions. Alabamians are justifiably famous for their "down home" cooking, with fried chicken dinners and shrimp dishes being prime examples. Fast-paced Birmingham is famous for its diverse culinary offerings, including numerous Greek and Italian restaurants. Visitors to the state's many food festivals can treat themselves to dishes made from such Alabama favorites as okra and muscadine grapes.

Mobile is home to traditional French, Spanish, and Creole cooking. Creole food draws on French and Spanish influences, as well as those of Africa and Haiti, to create the flavorful seafood stew called gumbo and the distinctive rice, shrimp,

DID YOU KNOW?

Cher amio [share a-MEE-oh] means "dear one" or "beloved" in the Creole French dialect.

▼ Revelers in Mobile have celebrated Mardi Gras since 1704.

and ham dish known as jambalaya. In 1952, Alabama country-music legend Hank Williams immortalized Creole jambalaya in his song of the same name.

Museums and Exhibits

Alabamians care a great deal about preserving their state's past and support state efforts to bring Alabama's cultural programs to a wide audience. Sightseeing opportunities exist all over the state. In the southern region, the Historic Mobile Preservation Society maintains exhibits on the American Civil War. In northern Alabama, the U.S. Space & Rocket Center in Huntsville demonstrates Alabamians' contributions to the nation's efforts to explore outer space. Among the many objects on display are a full-scale *Saturn V* rocket and the space shuttle *Pathfinder*. The Alabama Sports Hall of Fame in Birmingham exhibits mementos of such heroes as Olympic track star Jesse Owens and football legend Joe Namath. Anniston's Museum of Natural History spotlights Native American history and culture, as does the University of Alabama State Museum of Natural History in Tuscaloosa.

Tuskegee University's George Washington Carver Museum focuses on the cultural and artistic contributions of African Americans, including the famed Tuskegee Airmen. The National Voting Rights Museum and Institute in Selma

▲ Shuttle Park at the U.S. Space & Rocket Center in Huntsville features a full-scale model of the space shuttle.

◄ Students participate in the U.S. Space Camp in Huntsville, a five-day camp for fourth graders.

◀ An exhibit at the National Voting Rights Museum in Selma, founded by participants in the Selma-Montgomery March of 1965.

celebrates the Civil Rights Movement of the 1950s and 1960s. The Alabama Jazz Hall of Fame, devoted to a uniquely American musical style, can be found in Birmingham's historic Carver Theatre for the Performing Arts.

Painting, Sculpture, and More

The Birmingham Museum of Art has a diverse collection, including art from the American West and the Renaissance in Europe as well as the largest collection of Asian art in the southeastern United States. The Montgomery Museum of Fine Arts contains works by famous American painters such as Winslow Homer and John Singer Sargent, as well as the works of regional artists. Another Alabama site of interest for art lovers is the state capitol building in Montgomery. The capitol's central dome is covered with eight giant murals depicting scenes from Alabama's history. One of Alabama's most striking pieces of three-dimensional art is a massive statue of the Roman god Vulcan, which stands atop Red Mountain in southern Birmingham. This statue was Birmingham's contribution to the 1904 World's Fair and is the second largest statue in the nation, after the Statue of Liberty.

The Lively Arts

The Alabama Shakespeare Festival, begun in Anniston in 1972, is currently the fifth-largest annual event of its kind in the world. In addition to plays by William Shakespeare, the festival also presents the works of other playwrights, both classical and modern. The festival has made its home in Montgomery's performing arts complex since 1985.

Disputed Meteorite

In November 1954, Mrs. Ann Hodges of Sylacauga was lying asleep on her couch when an 8.5 pound (4 kilogram) meteorite crashed through the roof and hit her on the leg. The story of the only documented case of a meteorite hitting a person gets stranger. Mrs. Hodges's landlady claimed that the meteorite rightfully belonged to her, and the Alabama courts agreed. Mrs. Hodges was later able to buy the meteorite back, however, and she donated it to the Alabama Museum of Natural History. A fragment of the same meteorite was found by a farmer. That fragment is on display at the Hall of Meteorites at the National Museum of Natural History in Washington, D.C.

Established in 1947, the Birmingham Children's Theatre (BCT) is one of the nation's largest professional children's theaters. The BCT offers plays for young people from preschool through high school.

Alabama has a rich tradition of American music, from jazz, blues, and gospel to country and rock and roll. These musical forms are celebrated in annual festivals across the state, including the W. C. Handy Music Festival in Florence and the Tennessee Valley Old Time Fiddlers Convention at Athens State University in Athens. Classical music and opera are also well appreciated in Alabama. Concerts by Birmingham's Alabama Symphony Orchestra and the Huntsville Symphony Orchestra are well attended. Huntsville, Fort Payne, and Mobile are known for their opera companies.

The Media

Alabama has a long tradition of journalistic excellence. The state's largest-circulating, daily newspaper is the *Birmingham News*. Other influential Alabama newspapers include the *Huntsville Times*, the *Birmingham Post-Herald*, and the *Montgomery Advertiser*. The state's oldest newspaper still in print is the *Mobile Register*, which was established in 1813. In total, about 125 newspapers are published in Alabama, with about 25 published daily. Alabama boasts around 225 commercial radio and nearly three dozen television stations, as well as many superb public radio and television broadcasters. Birmingham is home to Alabama's first television station, WVTM-TV, which began operating in 1949 (as WAFM-TV). The nation's first state-owned educational television system, the Alabama Public Television Network, was established in 1955; today it includes several stations spread across the state and reaches every county in Alabama.

Literature

Alabama authors have made their mark on U.S. literature. One of the most famous is Harper Lee, who wrote the Pulitzer Prize-winning novel *To Kill a Mockingbird*. The daughter of a lawyer, Lee was born and raised in Alabama.

▲ A portrait of Hank Williams hangs in his Georgiana boyhood home, now a museum.

All That Jazz

The Alabama Jazz Hall of Fame in Birmingham honors the many world-class jazz artists associated with Alabama. Exhibits highlight the musical accomplishments of such luminaries as Nat "King" Cole, Duke Ellington, Lionel Hampton, and Erskine Hawkins. Visitors can travel from the beginnings of boogie-woogie with Clarence "Pinetop" Smith to the futuristic music of Sun Ra and his Intergalactic Space Arkestra.

The best-selling novel is based, in part, on her childhood experiences and explores race relations in the South in the 1930s. Lee shares a tie with another Alabama author, Truman Capote, who grew up in the state. Capote, author of the award-winning *In Cold Blood,* is generally considered the "father" of the true-crime genre. Harper Lee served as his research assistant for the book. Among Alabama's other well-known writers are Fannie Flagg, author of *Fried Green Tomatoes at the Whistle Stop Cafe,* and Winston Groom, who wrote *Forrest Gump.* The distinctive narrative voices of these writers illustrate the hopes and aspirations of Alabamians.

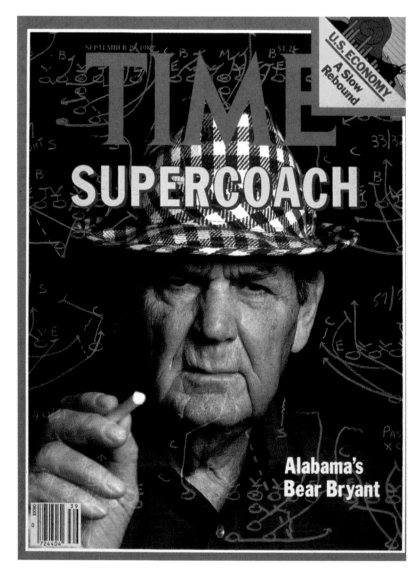

Sports

Alabamians are serious about sports, both as spectators and as participants. Although there are no major professional sports franchises in the state, there is no shortage of competitive play.

The University of Alabama's Crimson Tide and Auburn University's Tigers have a long-standing rivalry and vie for college football supremacy each year in a contest known as the Iron Bowl. Between 1958 and 1982, the Crimson Tide's legendary coach Paul "Bear" Bryant led his team to victory in six national college football championships. Each Christmas Day, Montgomery hosts the college Blue-Gray All Star Football Classic, drawing huge crowds. Mobile is home to the annual Senior Bowl, in which college senior football players strut their stuff in front of professional football scouts. Among the local football players who have

▲ Paul William Bryant was head coach at the University of Alabama from 1958 until his retirement in 1982. Bryant took his team to six national championships and fifteen bowl-game wins. He died about a month after his retirement.

"gone pro" are quarterbacks Bart Starr and Ken Stabler, receiver John Stallworth, and linebacker Kevin Greene.

Alabama is home to three minor-league baseball teams. The Huntsville Stars, the Birmingham Barons, and the Mobile Bay Bears serve as farm teams, respectively, for the Milwaukee Brewers, the Chicago White Sox, and the San Diego Padres. Outfielder Willie Mays and pitchers Leroy "Satchel" Paige and Don Sutton are among the baseball legends whose careers began on Alabama minor-league teams.

Golf is a popular pastime at the Robert Trent Jones Golf Trail, which winds through the state for more than 100 miles (161 km) and offers 378 holes of golfing. East of Birmingham lies the Talladega Superspeedway, a 2.66-mile (4.3-km) oval raceway where professional auto races, such as the Sears Diehard 500 and the Winston 500, are run each year. Stock car racing, in fact, is more popular than any other sport in Alabama except football. Greyhound racing is also a favored pursuit in such cities as Birmingham, Mobile, and Shorter.

▼ The Talladega Superspeedway is home to NASCAR's Winston 500 every October.

Able Alabamians

Nobler and grander than the child of Rome,
Curbing his chariot steeds,
The knightly scion of a Southern home
Dazzled the land with deeds.

*— from "John Pelham" by James Ryder Randall (1839–1908)
in An American Anthology, 1900, edited by
Edmund Clarence Stedman (1833–1908)*

Following are only a few of the thousands of people who were born, died, or spent much of their lives in Alabama and made extraordinary contributions to the state and the nation.

BOOKER T. WASHINGTON
EDUCATOR AND AUTHOR

BORN: *April 5, 1856, Franklin County, VA*
DIED: *November 14, 1915, Tuskegee*

As a child, Booker Taliaferro Washington worked in the West Virginia coal mines. In 1875, he graduated from the Hampton Institute in Virginia and six years later founded and became head of the Tuskegee Institute, an Alabama trade school. Its mission was to better the lives of African Americans. Washington led the Institute for twenty-five years, during which time the school's curriculum and student body greatly expanded. He believed the best way for African Americans to increase their status in society was through vocational training and financial stability. Washington was an influential fund-raiser for African-American causes and advised presidents Theodore Roosevelt and William Howard Taft on racial issues. He wrote many books, including his 1901 autobiography, *Up From Slavery*.

GEORGE WASHINGTON CARVER
SCIENTIST

BORN: *circa July 1861, near Diamond Grove, MO*
DIED: *January 5, 1943, Tuskegee*

A former slave, George Washington Carver worked his way through high school and college, eventually receiving both a bachelor's and master's degree in science. Carver then became head of the agriculture department at Alabama's Tuskegee Institute, where he researched the restoration of the Deep South's soil, which had been depleted by growing cotton. Carver had great success with soil management and crop rotation. Not only did he champion the cultivation of peanuts and soybeans, which restored the soil, he also found more than three hundred new uses for these crops, including the manufacture of plastics and inks. Carver's work helped to diversify southern agriculture and contributed to the economic rebirth of the South. Leaders around the world sought Carver's advice, and he received numerous awards for his many scientific achievements.

W.C. HANDY
MUSICIAN AND COMPOSER

BORN: *November 16, 1873, Florence*
DIED: *March 28, 1958, New York, NY*

Frequently hailed as the "Father of the Blues," African-American composer William Christopher Handy introduced blues music to white audiences. A cornet player and bandleader, Handy composed "Memphis Blues," "St. Louis Blues," and many other tunes. As a composer he used elements from many musical forms, including jazz, ragtime, and tango. Handy was also one of the first African-American music publishers. He relocated to New York City in the late 1910s and continued composing there, while arranging musical scores for

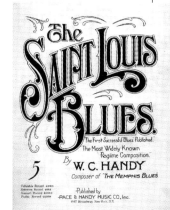

radio, film, and Broadway shows. He also wrote several books, including *Blues: An Anthology* (1926) and *Collection of Negro Spirituals* (1938).

HELEN KELLER
AUTHOR

BORN: *June 27, 1880, Tuscumbia*
DIED: *June 1, 1938, Westport, CT*

The daughter of a newspaper editor, Helen Adams Keller was rendered deaf and blind by a fever at the age of nineteen months. In 1887, Anne Sullivan began teaching Keller the manual alphabet, which consists of signs made into the hands of deaf-blind people. Keller went on to graduate with honors from Radcliffe College in 1904, where she wrote her best-selling autobiography, *The Story of My Life* (1902). She became a successful lecturer as well as an advocate for the disabled, a social reformer, and a suffragist. One of the first women inducted into the Alabama Women's Hall of Fame, Keller served as an inspiration to people everywhere.

JESSE OWENS
ATHLETE

BORN: *September 12, 1913, Danville*
DIED: *March 31, 1980, Tucson, AZ*

James Cleveland Owens was an African-American track and field athlete who shattered many world records. Owens set world records while only a senior in high school. He later distinguished himself at the 1936 Olympic Games in Berlin, where he won the running broad jump event and the 100-meter and 200-meter races and where he was a member of the victorious U.S. relay team. His victories at those games had a particular resonance because Adolph Hitler, whose Nazi regime ruled Germany at the time, believed in the superiority of the Aryan race. Owens received the Medal of Freedom from President Gerald Ford in 1976. Three years later, President Jimmy Carter honored him with the Living Legend Award. Owens was committed to the idea that athletics could be used to help resolve racial and political problems.

JOE LOUIS
BOXER

BORN: *May 13, 1914, Lafayette*
DIED: *April 12, 1981, Las Vegas, NV*

Born Joseph Louis Barrow, Joe Louis reigned as the world heavyweight champion in boxing from 1937 until his retirement in 1949. After winning many titles as an amateur, Louis began his professional career in 1934. On June 22, 1937, he defeated James J. Braddock to become the heavyweight champion. He remains the record-holder for having the longest reign as heavyweight champion. Louis was a highly skilled fighter known for his knockout punch; he ended his career with a total of fifty-four knockouts. Louis tried to return to boxing twice after his 1949 retirement but was defeated both times. After his death, Louis was awarded the American's Award by President Ronald Reagan in 1984.

NAT "KING" COLE
SINGER AND COMPOSER

BORN: *March 17, 1919, Montgomery*
DIED: *February 15, 1965, Santa Monica, CA*

Nathaniel Adams Cole was one of the first African-American popular singers to gain mainstream success and international fame. He was known not only for his smooth, romantic jazz vocal stylings but also for his outstanding piano skills. Cole's career took off in the 1940s, when he recorded extensively with his jazz group, the Nat King Cole Trio. Some of his best-known songs are "Mona Lisa" and "Unforgettable." Cole was the only African American to have his own network radio program in the 1940s, and he had his own television series from 1956 to 1957. Cole's appearances in concert halls, nightclubs, and on film brought him international stardom, and his records grossed more than $50 million.

HANK WILLIAMS
MUSICIAN AND COMPOSER

BORN: *September 17, 1923, Georgiana*
DIED: *January 1, 1953, Oak Hill, WV*

Hiram Williams began playing guitar at the age of eight. Influenced by gospel and country music, Williams began performing at a local radio station in the mid-1930s. His Nashville recording career yielded many hits, including "Honky Tonkin'" (1947) and "Move It On Over" (1947). "Lovesick Blues" was number one on the country charts for sixteen weeks in 1949. Although his songs made him a legend, Williams's drug and alcohol abuse led to his death at the age of twenty-nine. Today, Williams is considered the father of modern country music.

WILLIE MAYS
BASEBALL PLAYER

BORN: *May 6, 1931, Westfield*

After coming up from the Negro League and the minors, Willie Howard Mays, Jr., played center field for the New York (later San Francisco) Giants from 1951 to 1971, leaving baseball to serve in the U.S. Army from 1952 to 1954. Mays distinguished himself as a skilled fielder as well as a hitter, with 660 home runs to his credit by the end of his career. Mays was twice voted the National League's Most Valuable Player — in 1954 and 1965 — and played in twenty-four All-Star Games and four World Series. Mays went to the New York Mets in 1972 and retired the following year with a career total of 3,283 hits and a .302 batting average. Mays, a 1979 inductee into the National Baseball Hall of Fame, is considered one of the best players of all time.

HANK AARON
BASEBALL PLAYER

BORN: *February 5, 1934, Mobile*

Henry Louis Aaron started playing semi-professional baseball at the age of fifteen. After five years in the Negro Leagues and minor leagues, Aaron joined the Milwaukee Braves in 1954. Over the next twenty-three years, the African-American slugger earned the nickname "Hammerin' Hank." He retired with all-time records for home runs (755), runs batted in (2,297), and extra base hits (1,477), as well as three Gold Glove awards for fielding. Aaron spoke out against racism in baseball, accusing the sport of keeping African Americans out of management. Aaron was inducted into the National Baseball Hall of Fame in 1982. Today, Aaron works for the Turner Broadcasting System and mentors young baseball players on the farm teams of the Atlanta Braves.

MAE JEMISON
ASTRONAUT AND PHYSICIAN

BORN: *October 17, 1956, Decatur*

On September 12, 1992, Mae Carol Jemison became the first African-American woman to travel in space. Jemison served as a crew member aboard the shuttle *Endeavour*. Jemison earned an undergraduate degree in engineering from Stanford University and a medical degree from Cornell University. After working as a doctor for the Peace Corps in Africa, Jemison decided to become an astronaut. In 1988, Jemison completed her training and worked on shuttle software and mission preparation for U.S. spacecrafts. Jemison became part of the *Endeavour* flight team in 1992. Since then, Jemison, a 1993 inductee into the National Women's Hall of Fame, has taught at Dartmouth College and Cornell University and heads her own technology company.

Alabama
History At-A-Glance

1519
Alonso Alvarez de Piñeda sails into Mobile Bay.

1702
Fort Louis de la Mobile is founded on the Mobile River.

1763
France cedes present-day Alabama to Great Britain.

1780
Spain seizes Mobile from Great Britain.

1783
Great Britain gives northern and central regions of present-day Alabama to the United States and Mobile region to Spain.

1813
The United States seizes control of the Mobile area from Spain.

1817
The U.S. Congress establishes the Alabama Territory.

1819
Spain gives up its claim to lands north of the 42nd parallel and east of present-day Louisiana in the Adams–Onis Treaty.

1848
The "Alabama Platform," denying the federal government the right to outlaw slavery in the territories, is adopted.

1854
Alabama establishes its public school system.

1861
Alabama secedes from the Union and joins the Confederacy.

1864
Union forces win the Battle of Mobile Bay.

1600   **1700**   **1800**

1492
Christopher Columbus comes to New World.

1607
Capt. John Smith and three ships land on the Virginia coast and start first English settlement in New World — Jamestown.

1754–63
French and Indian War.

1773
Boston Tea Party.

1776
Declaration of Independence adopted July 4.

1777
Articles of Confederation adopted by Continental Congress.

1787
U.S. Constitution written.

1812–14
War of 1812.

United States
History At-A-Glance

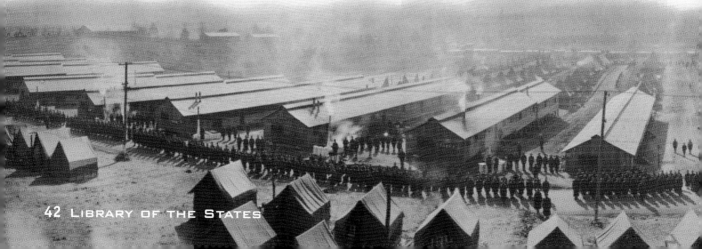

1868
Alabama rejoins the Union.

1881
Booker T. Washington establishes the Tuskegee Institute.

1901
Alabama adopts a new state constitution, which is still in use today.

1915
Alabama's cotton crop fails because of an infestation by the boll weevil.

1933
The federal government creates the Tennessee Valley Authority.

1946
U.S. Congress authorizes the construction of the Tennessee–Tombigbee Waterway.

1954
Dr. Martin Luther King, Jr., becomes pastor of Montgomery's Dexter Avenue Baptist Church.

1955
Rosa Parks refuses to give up her seat on a bus and sparks a bus boycott in Montgomery.

1963
Alabama governor George C. Wallace fails to stop racial integration at the University of Alabama.

1970
The Alabama (now U.S.) Space & Rocket Center opens in Huntsville.

1987
Guy Hunt becomes the first Republican governor of Alabama since 1874.

1992
Astronaut Mae Jemison is the first African-American woman in space.

1800   **1900**   **2000**

1848
Gold discovered in California draws eighty thousand prospectors in the 1849 Gold Rush.

1861–65
Civil War.

1869
Transcontinental railroad completed.

1917–18
U.S. involvement in World War I.

1929
Stock market crash ushers in Great Depression.

1941–45
U.S. involvement in World War II.

1950–53
U.S. fights in the Korean War.

1964–73
U.S. involvement in Vietnam War.

2000
George W. Bush wins the closest presidential election in history.

2001
A terrorist attack in which four hijacked airliners crash into New York City's World Trade Center, the Pentagon, and farmland in western Pennsylvania leaves thousands dead or injured.

▼ The 116th Infantry trained for World War I at Camp McClellan (now Fort McClellan) in northern Alabama.

Festivals and Fun for All

Check web site for exact date and directions.

Alabama National Fair and Agricultural Exposition, Montgomery

This mid-October event includes a circus, a petting zoo, pig races, carnival rides, livestock shows, student exhibits, and more.

www.alnationalfair.org

Big Spring Jam, Huntsville

Huntsville's annual downtown music festival is held each September with performances by nationally known musicians in various musical genres.

www.bigspringjam.org

Blue-Gray All Star Football Classic, Montgomery

Played every Christmas Day, this popular Alabama tradition draws huge crowds and is televised nationally.

www.bluegrayfootball.com

Chilton County Peach Festival, Clanton

Held every June to promote the local peach industry, festival events include beauty pageants, an art show, the Peach Parade, and the Peach Auction.

lcweb.loc.gov/bicentennial/propage/AL/al-3_h_riley2.html

City Stages, Birmingham

This May festival boasts 150 musical acts on ten stages.

www.citystages.org

Eufaula Pilgrimage, Eufaula

Each April, tours of historic homes are offered by the Eufaula Heritage Association.

www.zebra.net/~pilgrimage

Helen Keller Festival, Tuscumbia

This week-long celebration is held each June and offers arts and crafts, an art auction, puppet shows, and sporting events. The festival opens the season for outdoor performances of William Gibson's play *The Miracle Worker*.

www.helenkellerfestival.com

Historic Selma Pilgrimage & Antique Show, Selma

Every March Selma welcomes visitors for tours of historic homes, an antique show and sale, and a cemetery tour.

www.selmaalabama.com

NASCAR Winston 500, Talladega

One of the world's best-attended motor sport events, the NASCAR Winston Cup Series EA Sports™ 500 is run every

▲ Victorian Front Porch Christmas.

National Shrimp Festival, Gulf Shores
Established in 1971, this celebration of shellfish is held on the second weekend of October, Thursday through Saturday.
www.northbaldwinchamber.com/history/festivals2.html

Panoply, Huntsville
Held each April, Panoply is Huntsville's premiere festival of the visual and performing arts.
www.panoply.org

Poarch Creek Indian Intertribal Thanksgiving Day PowWow, Atmore
Held in late November at the Poarch Creek Indian Reservation, this event emphasizes Native American crafts, exhibitions, dance competitions, culture, and food.
Phone: 334-368-9136

Victorian Front Porch Christmas, Opelika
Held in December, this event invites visitors to view Opelika's historic houses and the art of Jan Jones, whose life-sized figures adorn the front porches of more than thirty century-old Alabama houses.
www.victorianfrontporch.com

W. C. Handy Music Festival, Florence
Occurring in late July or early August, this annual week-long musical celebration honors the life and work of Alabama jazz pioneer W. C. Handy.
www.wchandyfest.com

Zoo Weekend in Montgomery
Held in late March or early April, this fund-raiser for the Montgomery Zoo features games and animal rides.
www.zoo.ci.montgomery.al.us/events.htm

October at Talladega Superspeedway.
www.thatsracin.com

National Peanut Festival, Dothan
Held each fall, this event celebrating the peanut includes livestock shows, a milking contest, homemaking exhibits, youth exhibits, recipe contests, bowling, tennis, karate, and a choral festival. It draws more than 163,000 visitors annually.
www.nationalpeanutfestival.com

Books

Keller, Helen. *The Story of My Life*. New York: Bantam, 1991. Helen Keller's autobiography, originally published in 1902.

Wilkie, Curtis. *Dixie: A Personal Odyssey through Events That Shaped the Modern South*. New York: Scribner, 2001. An account of the history of the South intended for older readers.

Wills, Charles A. *A Historical Album of Alabama*. Danbury, CT: Millbrook Press, 1995. The history of Alabama from its early settlement to the present day.

Wilson, Camilla. *Rosa Parks: From the Back of the Bus to the Front of a Movement*. New York: Scholastic, 2001. This biography for young readers examines Parks's life up to and after her fateful bus trip.

Web Sites

▶ The official state site
www.state.al.us/2k1

▶ The official state capital site
www.montgomery.al.us

▶ Alabama History On-Line
www.archives.state.al.us/aho.html

▶ Alabama museums
www.museumca.org/usa/al.html

Films

Anker, Daniel and Barak Goodman. *Scottsboro: An American Tragedy*. Boston: WGBH/American Experience, 2001.

McCabe, Daniel and Paul Stekler. *George Wallace: Settin' the Woods on Fire*. Boston: WGBH/American Experience, 2000.

Mulligan, Robert. *To Kill a Mockingbird*. Los Angeles: Universal Studios, 1962. The classic film version of Harper Lee's book.

Note: Page numbers in *italics* refer to maps, illustrations, or photographs.

N
Namath, Joe, 33
Narváez, Pánfilo de, 8
NASCAR Winston 500, 45
National Association for the Advancement of Colored People (NAACP), 15
National Peanut Festival, 44
National Shrimp Festival, 45
National Voting Rights Museum, 33–34, *34*
Native Americans, 4, 8, 9–11, 17, 45
Natural Bridge, 20
natural resources, 4, 7, 20
newspapers, 35
nut (state), 6

O
opera, 35
Owens, Jesse, 33, 39–40

P
Paige, Leroy "Satchel," 37
Panoply, 45
parks, *23*
Parks, Rosa McCauley, 15, *15*
Perdido Bay, 21
Pierce, Franklin, 31
Pinckney, Thomas, 10
Piñeda, Alonso Alvarez de, 8
plants, 23
Poarch Creek Indian Intertribal Thanksgiving Day PowWow, 45
politics and political figures
Bibb, William Wyatt, 11, 28
Goldwater, Barry M., 31
governmental structure, 28–31
Harrison, William Henry, 11
Hunt, Guy, 31
Jackson, Andrew, 10–11
James, Forest "Fob," 31

King, William Rufus de Vane, 30
Kolb, Reuben F., 24
Lincoln, Abraham, 11, 28
Pinckney, Thomas, 10
Wallace, George C., 31, *31*
Yancey, William L., 11
Pope, John, 28
population, 6, 16, 17–18
Populist movement, 24

R
racial issues, 31
racial makeup of Alabama, 17
rainfall, 21
Reconstruction, 12–13
recreation, 27
Red Eagle (William Weatherford), *10,* 10–11
Red Mountain, 7, 34
Redstone Arsenal, 14–15
religion, 19
reptile (state), 6
Republican Party, 31
Revolutionary War, 10
rivers, 21–23
Russell Cave National Monument, 7

S
St. Stephens, Alabama, 11
Samford University, 19
Scottsboro, Alabama, 7
seal of Alabama, 28
secession, 11–12, 28
segregation, 15, 19, 31
Selma Pilgrimage and Antique Show, 45
Senate, 30
Senior Bowl, 36
service industry, 26
settlers, 8–10, 16–17
Shawnee Indians, 10
shell (state), 6
Shuttle Park, *33*

slavery, 11–12, 17, 28
snowfall, 21
song (state), 6
Soto, Hernando de, 8
space program, 14, 15
Spanish explorers, 9, 10
sports, 36–37, 39–41
Stabler, Ken, 37
Stallworth, John, 37
Starr, Bart, 37
state legislature, 30
statehood, 6, 11, 17, 24
Sutton, Don, 37

T
Talladega Superspeedway, *37*
Tallapoosa River, 21
Tecumseh, 10, 11, *11*
temperature, 21
Tennessee River, 21
Tennessee River Valley, 20
Tennessee-Tombigbee Waterway, 26
Tennessee Valley Authority (TVA), 14
Tennessee Valley Old Time Fiddlers Convention, 35
Tensaw River, 21
Tenskwatawa, 11
time line of Alabama history, 42–43
To Kill a Mockingbird (Lee), 35–36
Tombigbee River, 9, 11, 21, 23
tourism, 27
Treaty of San Lorenzo, 10
tree (state), 6
Tuscaloosa, Alabama, 29
Tuskeegee Airmen, *7,* 7, 33
Tuskeegee University, 19, 33

U
Unclaimed Baggage, 7
University of Alabama, 36

University of Alabama State Museum of Natural History, 33
University of Alabama system, 19, 31
U.S. Space & Rocket Center, 7, 33, *33*

V
Vespucci, Amerigo, 8
Victorian Front Porch Christmas, 45, *45*
Voting Rights Act (1965), 15

W
W. C. Handy Music Festival, 35, 45
Waldseemüller, Martin, 8
Wallace, George C., 31, *31*
War of 1812, 11
Washington, Booker T., 4, 38, *38*
waterways, 5
Weatherford, William (Red Eagle), *10,* 10-11
Wheeler Lake, 23
wildlife, *21,* 23
Wilkinson, James, 10
Williams, Hank, 4, 32, 33, *35,* 40–41
World War I, 13
World War II, 14–15

Y
Yancey, William L., 11

Z
Zoo Weekend in Montgomery, 45